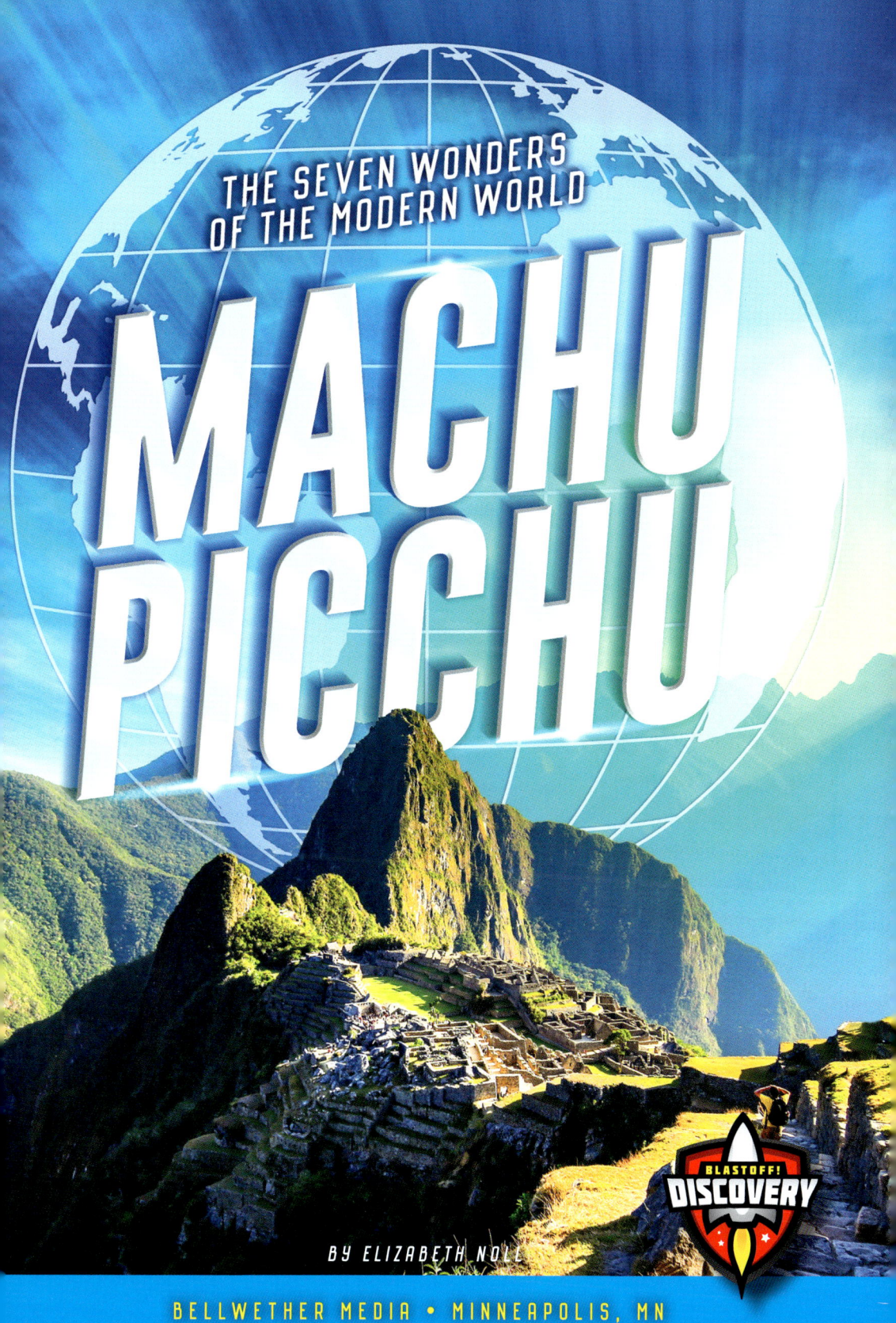

Blastoff! Discovery launches a new mission: reading to learn. Filled with facts and features, each book offers you an exciting new world to explore!

This edition first published in 2021 by Bellwether Media, Inc.

No part of this publication may be reproduced in whole or in part without written permission of the publisher. For information regarding permission, write to Bellwether Media, Inc., Attention: Permissions Department, 6012 Blue Circle Drive, Minnetonka, MN 55343.

Library of Congress Cataloging-in-Publication Data

Names: Noll, Elizabeth, author.
Title: Machu Picchu / by Elizabeth Noll.
Description: Minneapolis, MN : Bellwether Media, Inc., 2021. |
Series: Blastoff discovery!: The Seven Wonders of the Modern World
 | Includes bibliographical references and index. | Audience: Ages 7-13 | Audience: Grades 4-6 | Summary: "Engaging images accompany information about Machu Picchu. The combination of high-interest subject matter and narrative text is intended for students in grades 3 through 8"– Provided by publisher.
Identifiers: LCCN 2020018900 (print) | LCCN 2020018901 (ebook) | ISBN 9781644872697 (library binding) | ISBN 9781681037325 (ebook)
Subjects: LCSH: Machu Picchu Site (Peru)–Juvenile literature. | Inca architecture–Juvenile literature.
Classification: LCC F3429.1.M3 N65 2021 (print) | LCC F3429.1.M3 (ebook) | DDC 985/.37–dc23
LC record available at https://lccn.loc.gov/2020018900
LC ebook record available at https://lccn.loc.gov/2020018901

Text copyright © 2021 by Bellwether Media, Inc. BLASTOFF! DISCOVERY and associated logos are trademarks and/or registered trademarks of Bellwether Media, Inc.

Editor: Betsy Rathburn   Designer: Brittany McIntosh

Printed in the United States of America, North Mankato, MN.

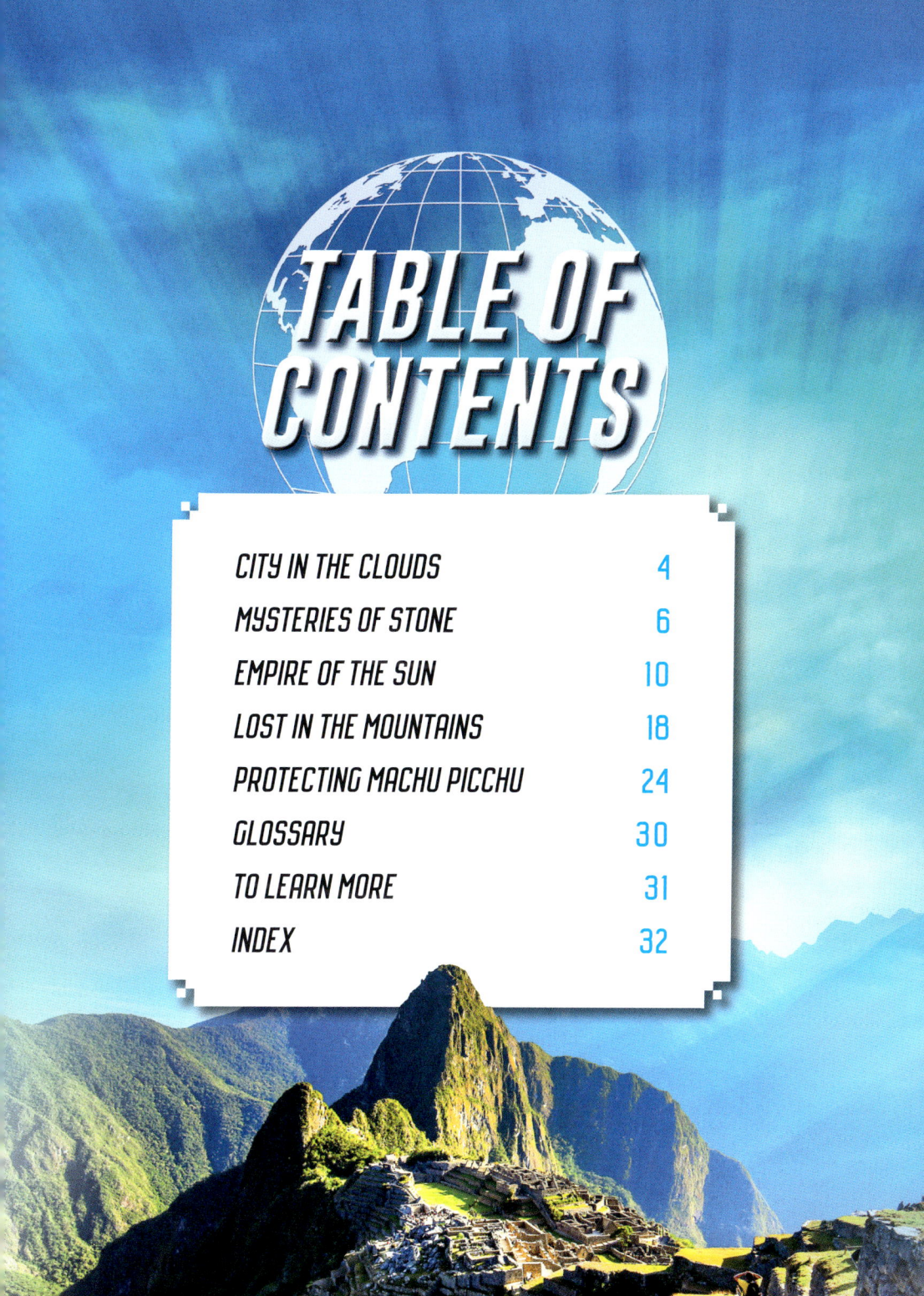

TABLE OF CONTENTS

CITY IN THE CLOUDS	4
MYSTERIES OF STONE	6
EMPIRE OF THE SUN	10
LOST IN THE MOUNTAINS	18
PROTECTING MACHU PICCHU	24
GLOSSARY	30
TO LEARN MORE	31
INDEX	32

CITY IN THE CLOUDS

You have been hiking the Inca Trail for days. This path through the mountains of Peru reaches heights of more than 10,000 feet (3,048 meters). It passes through a high **cloud forest**. At this **altitude**, there is less oxygen in the air than you are used to. It is hard to catch your breath.

   The path begins to wind around the mountain. You step on wide stone slabs. Suddenly, a wonderful sight appears before you. It is a green meadow filled with stone buildings. It is surrounded by nearby peaks and clouds. You are looking at Machu Picchu!

MYSTERIES OF STONE

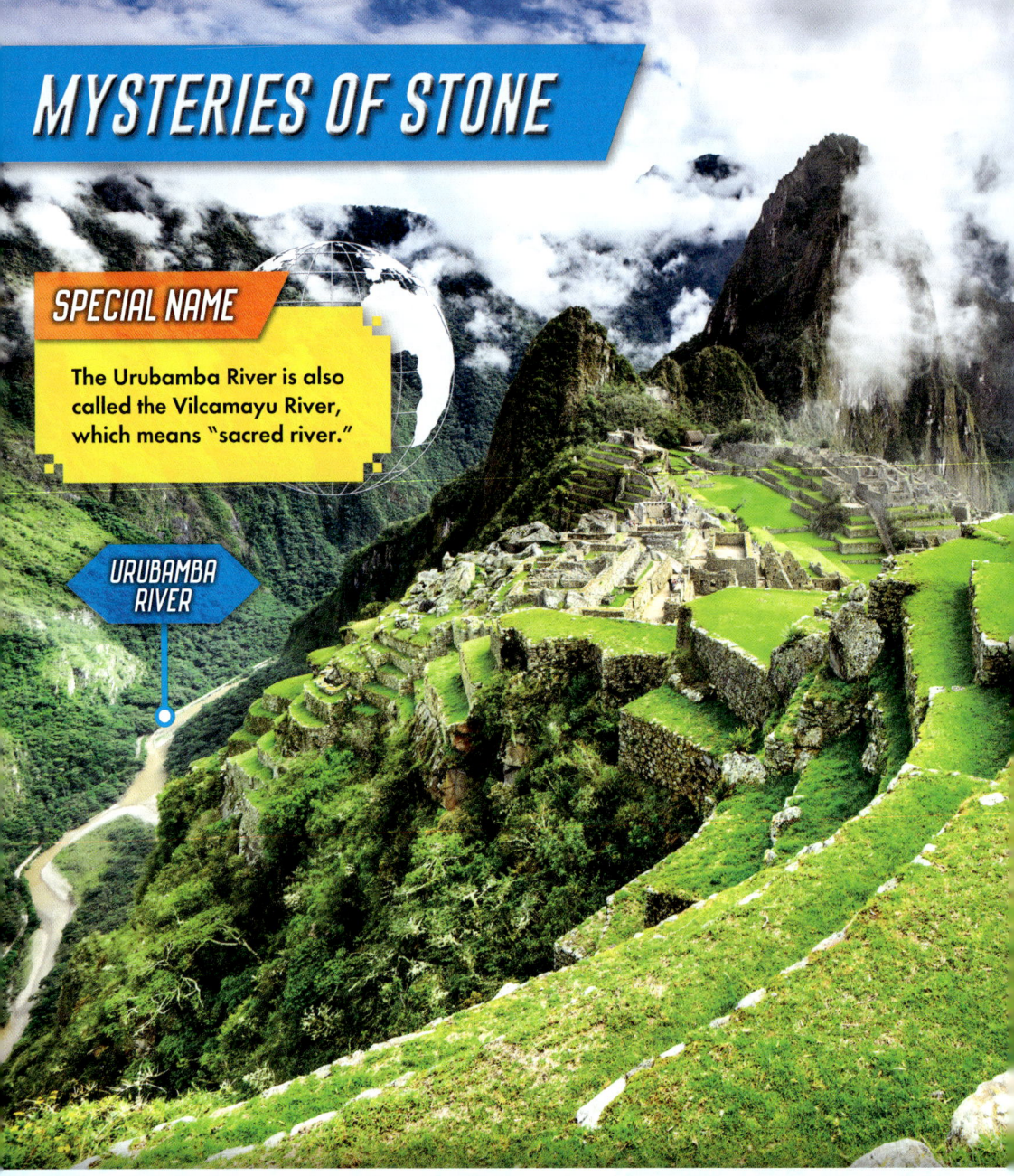

SPECIAL NAME

The Urubamba River is also called the Vilcamayu River, which means "sacred river."

URUBAMBA RIVER

Machu Picchu is a ruin in Peru. It is almost 600 years old. The ruins lie high in the Andes Mountains. These peaks run along Peru's coastline. The mountains are so high that their tops are in the clouds. Machu Picchu is close to the mountaintop.

A mountain called Huayna Picchu rises above the ruins. Far below, the Urubamba River bends around the mountain. In the distance, other mountain peaks are visible.

HUAYNA PICCHU

WHERE IS MACHU PICCHU?

MACHU PICCHU
PERU

Machu Picchu is famous for its **terraces**. These grass-covered ledges look like huge steps carved into the mountainside. There are more than 700 in total! The ancient city is also home to more than 1,000 steps. These stone-carved steps lead to more than 200 structures throughout the city.

TERRACES

TEMPLE OF THE SUN

GOLDEN WALLS

At one time, the walls in the Temple of the Sun were covered in sheets of gold!

There are many temples in Machu Picchu. One of the most famous is the Temple of the Sun. It is made of many light-colored stones stacked on top of each other. The Temple of the Moon is also well known. It is inside a mountain cave. Other structures include **tombs** and royal homes.

TEMPLE OF THE MOON

EMPIRE OF THE SUN

In the 1400s, the Inca people gained power in the Andes Mountains. Their empire soon stretched for thousands of miles. It included 12 million people! The capital was Cusco. Up to 150,000 people lived there at its peak.

CUSCO

HONORING INTI

No one knows for sure why Machu Picchu was built. Many scientists think it was a royal retreat for an Inca emperor named Pachacuti. Others think Machu Picchu was built for religious purposes. The city in the clouds may have honored the sun god Inti.

PACHACUTI

AQUEDUCT

The Inca were excellent **engineers**. They built more than 25,000 miles (40,234 kilometers) of stone roads to connect their empire. They built **aqueducts** and **canals** to carry water to their cities.

The Inca used their engineering knowledge to build Machu Picchu. They built an aqueduct to bring water to the city from a nearby spring. The water ran to Pachacuti's house first. Then it ran to other houses and fountains.

FOUNTAIN

THEN AND NOW

THEN

The Inca built long aqueducts to bring water to Machu Picchu from a nearby spring. Slopes helped the water move.

NOW

Aqueducts are still used today! Water is now carried to a water treatment plant, where it is made safe to drink. Machines often help the water move.

The Inca also learned how to farm on the steep mountainside. There was no flat land to build houses or grow crops. There was also no way to stop **erosion** that could destroy the city over time. The Inca terrace system solved these problems.

Builders used large stones to make the **foundation** of the terraces. Then, they covered the stones with small rocks and soil from the valley below.

FOUNDATION

TERRACES

1. Workers dug a flat area into the mountain. They made a foundation out of large stones.

2. Workers added smaller stones on top of the foundation. Then they added a layer of small gravel.

3. Workers covered the rock with rich soil from the valley below. Now the terrace was ready for farming!

The Inca are also famous for their **masonry**. Many believe they learned it from groups they conquered, such as the Tiwanaku and the Wari. The Inca collected stones from **quarries** below the Machu Picchu building site. They pushed the heavy stones along sloped roads up the mountain. Then, they used stronger rocks to pound the stones into shape.

MACHU PICCHU TIMELINE

1100s CE
The Inca capital is established in Cusco

1400s
The Inca Empire spreads rapidly

AROUND 1450
The Inca begin building Machu Picchu

1500s
Machu Picchu is abandoned

1532
The Spanish arrive in the Inca Empire

1911
Hiram Bingham III finds Machu Picchu

HISTORY'S MYSTERIES

Scientists still do not know how the Inca carved stones that fit so closely together. The huge rocks were not easy to move!

The stones fit closely together with no **mortar**. They fit together so closely that a sheet of paper cannot fit between them! These carefully shaped, interlocking rocks have held together for centuries. Even earthquakes have not toppled Machu Picchu's stones!

LOST IN THE MOUNTAINS

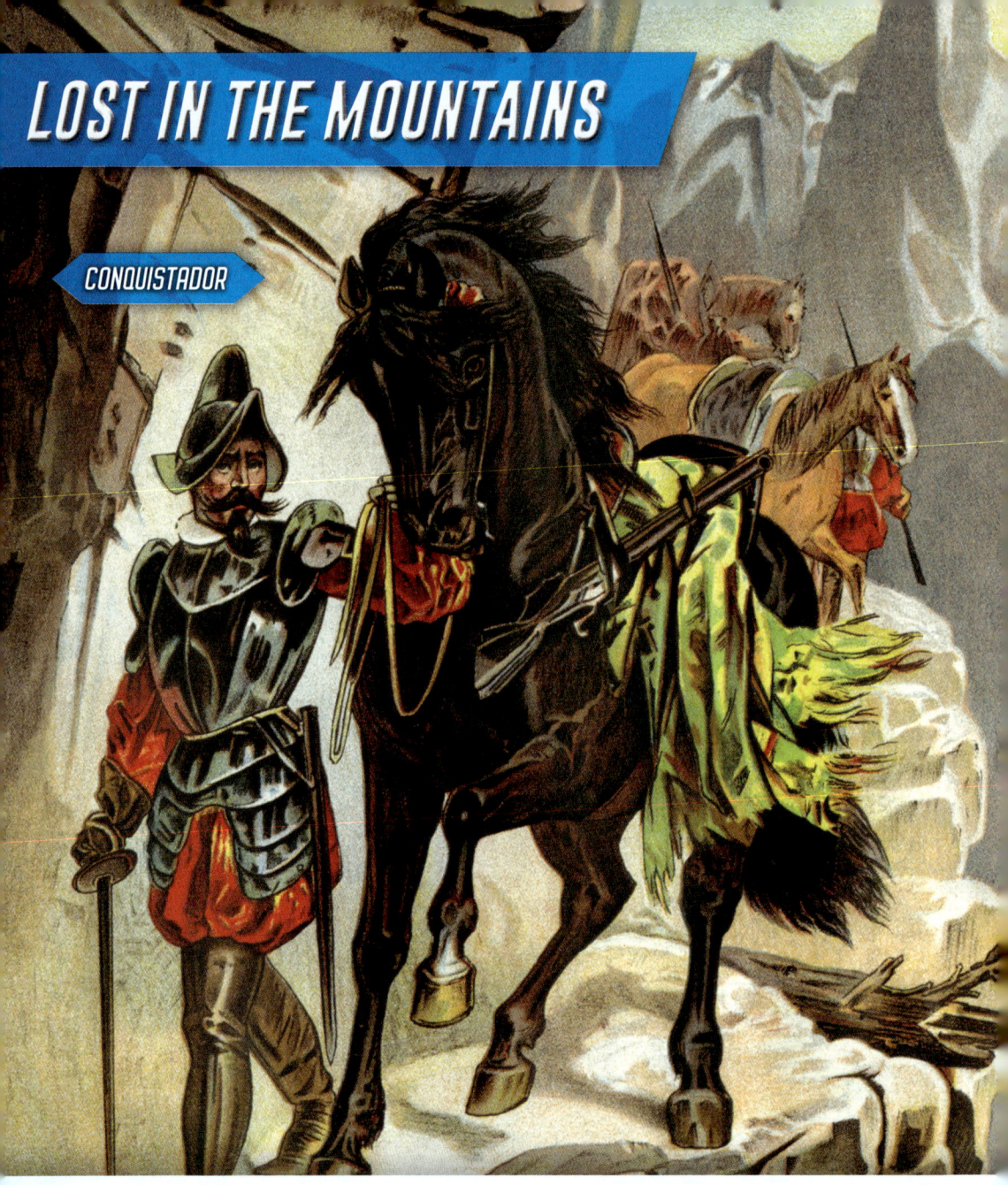

CONQUISTADOR

People only lived at Machu Picchu for about 100 years. The city in the clouds was abandoned sometime in the 1500s. Nobody is sure of the reason.

In the early decades of the 1500s, Spanish **conquistadors** explored South America. They attacked the Inca and other people living there. Many **indigenous** people died in these battles. Even more may have been killed by diseases carried by the Spanish soldiers.

The Spanish invaders destroyed many important Inca temples and cities. But they never found Machu Picchu. For more than 400 years, it remained undisturbed in the clouds at the top of the mountain. Only locals knew about it.

In 1911, Hiram Bingham III went looking for the lost Inca city of Vilcabamba. He brought a group of scientists with him to Cusco. A guide named Melchor Arteaga led him to the terraces where modern farmers were using them to grow crops. A local boy led him farther still, all the way up to the ruins of Machu Picchu.

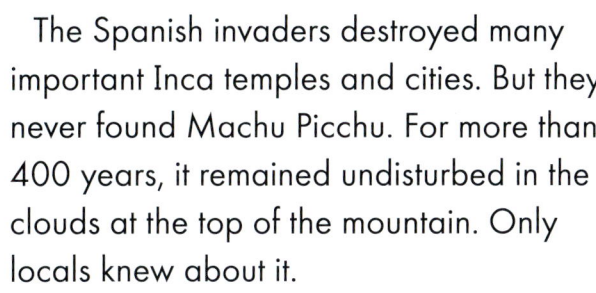
HIRAM BINGHAM III

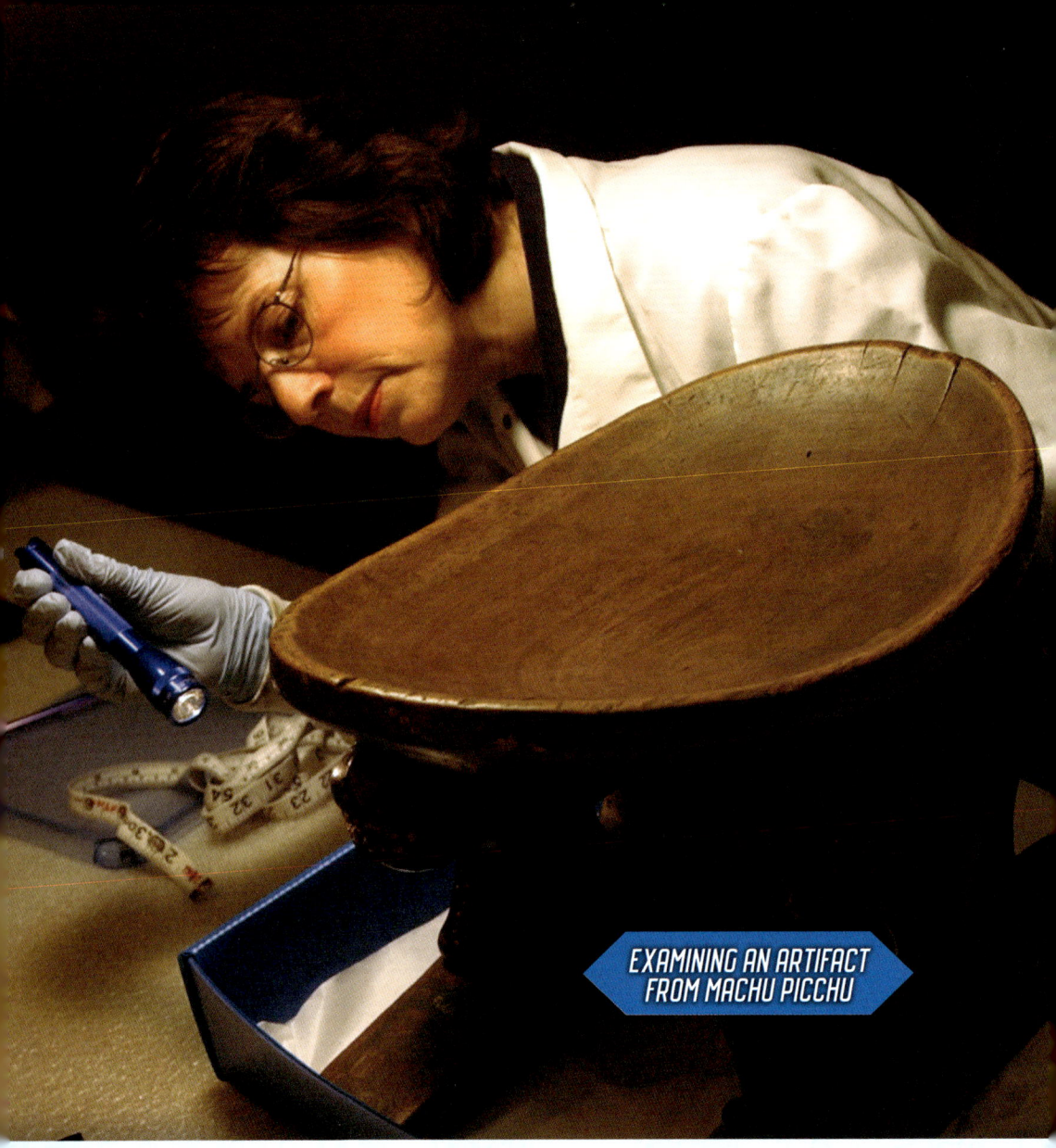

EXAMINING AN ARTIFACT FROM MACHU PICCHU

For the next several years, Bingham returned to Machu Picchu with other scientists. They cleared away the jungle plants that had grown over the stone houses and temples. They took measurements and photographs. They also dug up **artifacts**. They found pots and jewelry. They even found caves where people had been buried!

Bingham took thousands of artifacts from Machu Picchu back to Yale University. He put them in the museum there. But people in Peru wanted the artifacts back. They were part of the country's history. In 2011, 100 years after Bingham first saw Machu Picchu, the artifacts were finally returned!

MACHU PICCHU MUSEUM IN CUSCO

THINK ABOUT IT

If a foreign archaeologist digs up artifacts in a different country, which country should the artifacts belong to? Why?

PROTECTING MACHU PICCHU

In 2007, Machu Picchu was named a Wonder of the Modern World. It is also a **UNESCO** World Heritage site. More than 1 million people visit Machu Picchu every year. **Tourism** helps Peru make money. But visitors can cause serious problems at Machu Picchu. **Pollution** and erosion also cause many issues.

Maintenance teams work to repair and protect Machu Picchu. The Peruvian government has also made new rules to help preserve the site for the future. They limit the number of visitors who can be at the ruins at one time. They also limit how much time people can spend there.

MAINTENANCE WORKER

TOURISTS VISITING MACHU PICCHU

People are still making discoveries at Machu Picchu. In 2017, **archaeologists** found a room with a paved stone floor inside one of the buildings. In one corner of the stone floor were pieces of a broken jar. The scientists think the jar is about 500 years old!

POP CULTURE CONNECTION

MOVIE: *The Emperor's New Groove*
YEAR: 2000
DESCRIPTION: The main character, Kuzco, is the emperor of the Inca Empire. When he is turned into a llama, he must rely on the help of others to be changed back. The movie is based on the real-life Inca Empire. Filmmakers traveled to Machu Picchu to study the Inca people and find inspiration.

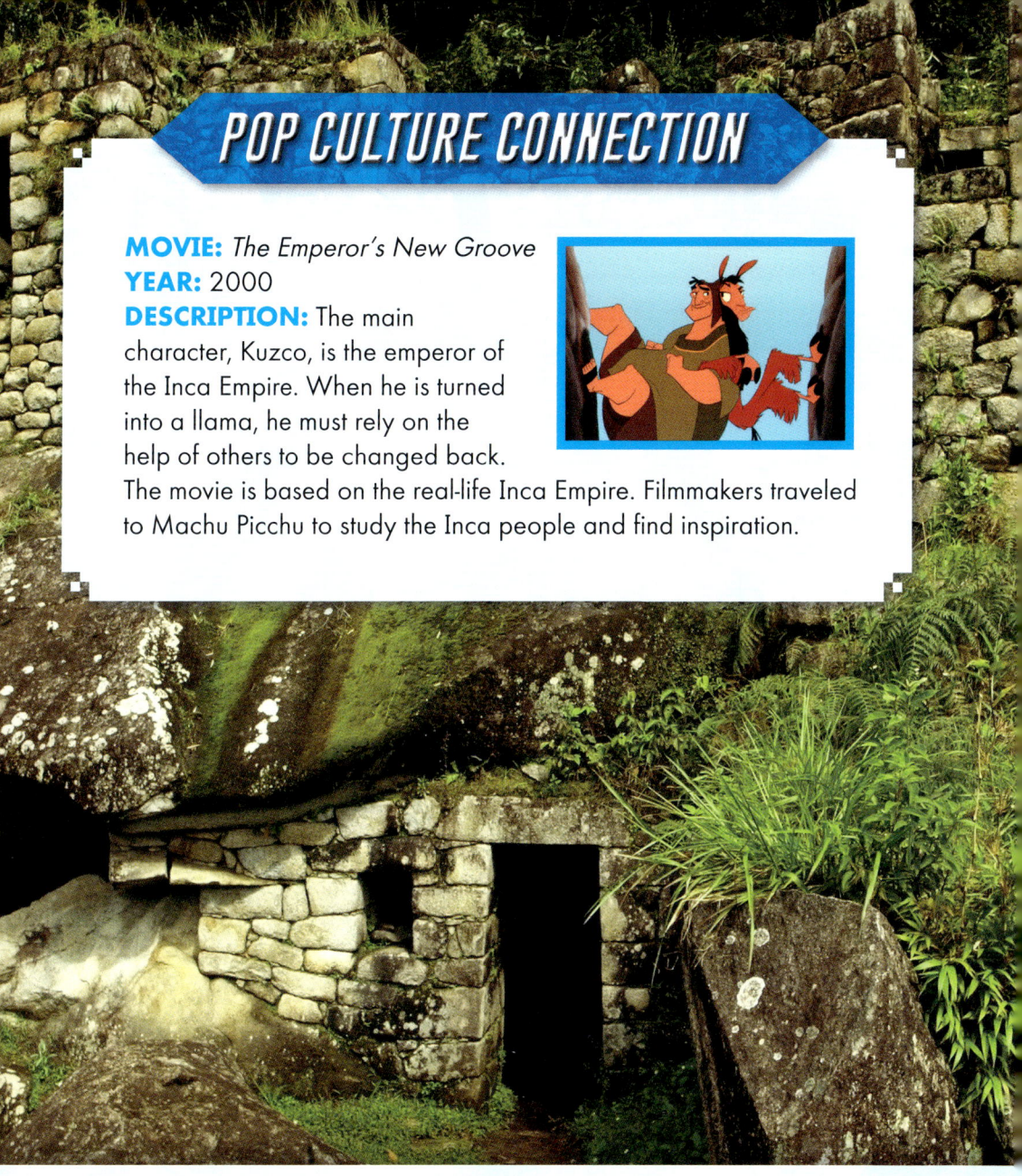

Near the stone floor is a room with two large containers. Archaeologists believe that the Inca people poured water into the containers and studied the stars that were reflected in the water. These are called water mirrors!

Many companies offer tours of Machu Picchu. Some bring visitors along the Inca Trail. This four-day hike from Cusco is open almost every month of the year. Visitors see many Inca ruins. They also pass cliffs and waterfalls. Some tour groups are making Machu Picchu more accessible. In 2019, a new tour company began offering tours for wheelchair users.

COMPARE AND CONTRAST

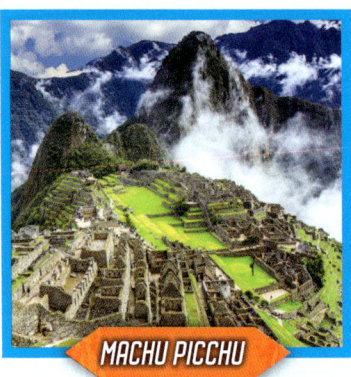
MACHU PICCHU

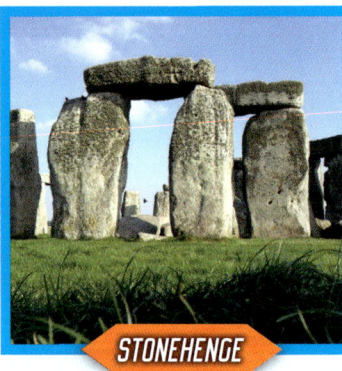
STONEHENGE

LOCATION
Peru

BUILT
around 1450 CE

SIZE
126 square miles
(326 square kilometers)

PURPOSE
retreat for Pachacuti,
religious use

LOCATION
England

BUILT
around 3000 to 1520 BCE

SIZE
10 square miles
(26 square kilometers)

PURPOSE
religious use, burial

Machu Picchu is an important **symbol** of Peru. It preserves the history of the Inca Empire. People around the world travel a long way to see this modern wonder!

GLOSSARY

altitude—the height that a place reaches

aqueducts—human-made channels that bring water from one place to another

archaeologists—scientists who study things left behind by ancient people

artifacts—items made long ago by humans; artifacts tell people today about people from the past.

canals—human-made waterways that drain or irrigate land or help people get around

cloud forest—a mountain forest located in a warm area, often with many clouds

conquistadors—leaders of Spanish conquests in the Americas during the 16th century

engineers—people who design things to be built

erosion—the process through which rocks are worn away by wind, water, ice, or human activity

foundation—a base or support on top of which a structure is built

indigenous—related to the people who first lived in an area

masonry—stonework

mortar—a building material that hardens when it dries; mortar is used to fill cracks.

pollution—the presence of harmful materials in the environment

quarries—places from which rocks are dug for use in building

symbol—something that stands for something else

terraces—flat ridges on a hillside that help keep the soil in place

tombs—structures that hold the remains of people who have passed away

tourism—the business of people traveling to visit other places

UNESCO—the United Nations Educational, Scientific and Cultural Organization; UNESCO works to educate people and preserve world landmarks.

TO LEARN MORE

AT THE LIBRARY

Jackson, Tom. *Eyewitness: Wonders of the World*. New York, N.Y.: DK Publishing, 2014.

Klepeis, Alicia Z. *Peru*. Minneapolis, Minn.: Bellwether Media, 2019.

Stine, Megan. *Where Is Machu Picchu?* New York, N.Y.: Penguin Workshop, 2018.

ON THE WEB

Factsurfer.com gives you a safe, fun way to find more information.

1. Go to www.factsurfer.com.
2. Enter "Machu Picchu" into the search box and click 🔍.
3. Select your book cover to see a list of related content.

INDEX

Andes Mountains, 6, 10
aqueducts, 12, 13
archaeologists, 26, 27
Arteaga, Melchor, 21
artifacts, 22, 23, 26, 27
Bingham III, Hiram, 21, 22, 23
canals, 12
compare and contrast, 28
construction, 13, 15, 16, 17
Cusco, 10, 21, 23, 28
discoveries, 26, 27
Emperor's New Groove, The, 27
erosion, 14, 24
Huayna Picchu, 7
Inca, 10, 11, 12, 13, 14, 16, 17, 19, 21, 27, 28
Inca Empire, 10, 29
Inca Trail, 4, 28
location, 6, 7
masonry, 16, 17
Pachacuti, 11, 13
Peru, 4, 6, 23, 24, 29
pollution, 24
pop culture connection, 27
purpose, 11
quarries, 16
Spanish, 19, 21
Temple of the Moon, 9
Temple of the Sun, 9
temples, 9, 21, 22
terraces, 8, 14, 15, 21
then and now, 13
think about it, 23
timeline, 16
tourism, 24, 25, 28
UNESCO, 24
Urubamba River, 6, 7

The images in this book are reproduced through the courtesy of: Roberto Ragusa, front cover, pp. 3, 31; sharptoyou, pp. 4-5; cge2010, p. 5; Don Mammoser, pp. 6 (top), 14; Anton_Ivanov, p. 7 (bottom); amadeustx, p. 8; Cristian E Rodriguez, p. 9 (top); Ecuadorpostales, p. 9 (bottom); National Geographic Image Collection/ Alamy, pp. 10, 15 (top), 20; Pictures Now/ Alamy, p. 11 (top); lovelypeace, p. 11 (bottom); Lena Kuhnt/ Alamy, p. 12; Timothy Mulholland/ Alamy, p. 13 (top); Michal Sikorski/ Alamy, p. 13 (then); Javani LLC, p. 13 (now); Daniel Prudek, p. 13 (bottom); Ivan_off, p. 15 (step 1); TOON DANUCHOT, p. 15 (step 2); Alexey Stiop, p. 15 (step 3); NiarKrad, p. 15 (bottom); Reciprocity Images/ Alamy, p. 16; Jack Young - Places/ Alamy, p. 17; North Wind Picture Archives/ Alamy, pp. 18, 19; Rapp Halour/ Alamy, p. 21; Kathryn Scott Osler/ Getty Images, p. 22; PRISMA ARCHIVO/ Alamy, p. 23 (top); robertharding/ Alamy, p. 23 (bottom); Benjamin Phelan/ Alamy, p. 24; Matyas Rehak, p. 25; Jim Wileman/ Alamy, pp. 26, 29; Photo 12/ Alamy, p. 27 (top); Dave Rock, p. 27 (bottom); emperorcosar, p. 28 (Machu Picchu); Ayten Hologlu, p. 28 (Stonehenge); Gleb Aitov, p. 28 (bottom).